PIE FORTUNE
and the
GOLDEN LAMP

PIE FORTUNE
and the
GOLDEN LAMP

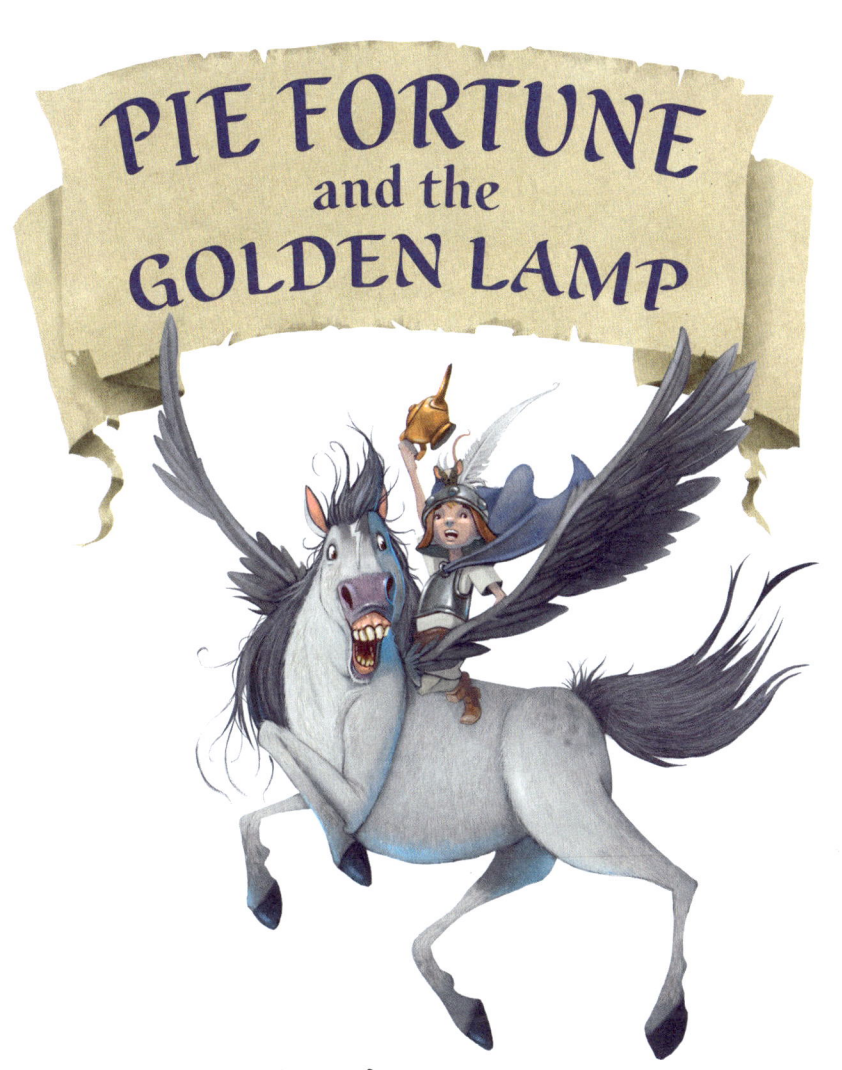

Gareth P Jones
Dan Whisker

Collins

Contents

Meet the three heroes! 2
Chapter 1 Lightning the Winged Horse 4
Lightning the Wonder Horse! 14
Chapter 2 The Golden Lamp
   of Kabbam 16
The Kingdom of Mirthia 28
Chapter 3 Big Chicken Express 30
Breaking news! 42
Chapter 4 The half a hole 44
Captain Bushybeard's memoir 54
Chapter 5 What goes down must go up 56
Mantini's act 68
Chapter 6 The enor-mouse 70
Commander Nelson's Brilliant
   Defence Plan 82
Captain Bushybeard's notebook 84
About the author 86
About the illustrator .88
Book chat 90

Meet the three heroes!

PIE FORTUNE
INTELLIGENCE: 9/10
MAIN STRENGTH: Intelligence/wit
CURRENT JOB: Wildlife Safari Park Ranger

AGNES MAGPIE
INTELLIGENCE: 8/10
STRENGTH: Magic (when it works)
JOB: Royal Magic Advisor

CLAYMORE (THE DREADED HOOD)
INTELLIGENCE: 4/10
STRENGTH: Fighting
CURRENT JOB: Dishwasher

Chapter 1

Lightning the Winged Horse

Pie Fortune breathed in the fresh air and looked up at the blue sky. He loved his new job of Wildlife Safari Park Ranger.

On his first day, Gertrude Porter, the chief ranger, had led him on a brisk stroll around the outer fence.

"There are rather a lot of holes in it," said Pie.

"Oh, I can see you're as sharp as a sabre-toothed beaver's teeth," said Gertrude. She had a no-nonsense approach. She stepped through a hole so large, she didn't even need to duck.

"Do you want me to mend them?" asked Pie. "I repaired a lot of fences when I worked as a shepherd."

"Of course not. How will the animals be able to get in if there aren't any holes?"

"Get in?" said Pie, confused.

"Yes. Our visitors don't pay for the chance to see a few mangy pigeons." Gertrude flapped her arms to scare away a couple of birds.

"But isn't the fence supposed to keep them in?" said Pie.

"They're wild animals," said Gertrude. "They come and go. Your job is to fill the food bowls every morning around the park to lure them inside. I just hope you're more suited to the role than the last few rangers we've had. I say, you're not the sort of person who is likely to get eaten, are you?" She looked at him quizzically.

"I don't think so. I've never been eaten before. Oh, except for one time, but that was on purpose. You see, I was working for a troll barber when one of our regulars swallowed the – "

"Never mind that," Gertrude interrupted, impatiently. "I'd rather you avoided getting eaten if you wouldn't mind. It's extremely annoying having to employ new rangers all the time."

"I can imagine," said Pie.

Pie spent the next few days happily wandering around, filling the food bowls, and avoiding being eaten by the animals who did enter. It felt good to be working in the great outdoors, following his previous three jobs.

His role as overnight cupboard cleaner had been dark, dusty and lonely. The job as an executioner's blindfold tester had been bruising and confusing. After that, he took a job sweeping up after a dragon. It was kept under the royal palace to provide the king's bathroom with underfloor heating.

That job had come to a sudden end when the door had been left unlocked, allowing the dragon to escape.

A park ranger was a definite improvement. Pie had always believed that animals should be free, so he appreciated this fresh new approach to running a wildlife park. Gertrude was pleased with his efforts and Pie was happy in his work.

"Did you see, we had a rhinonkersaurus in today, as well as a flock of nibbling gull-bats?" Gertrude said, at the end of the third day. "Almost all of the visitors seemed very pleased."

"Almost all?" said Pie.

"Well, one got eaten, but it was his own fault for trying to pet the rhinonkersaurus."

And then, following a quiet couple of days, Pie's boss made a decision that changed everything.

"This is no good, at all," said Gertrude, shaking her head as she studied the visitors' book. "We had three and a half visitors today and – "

"What do you mean 'a half'?" interrupted Pie.

"One was a child. But that's not the point. They were here all day and the only wildlife they saw were two sparrows and a worm. And then one of the sparrows ate the worm. If we get another bad review on that visitors' board in the marketplace, it'll be the end of this place."

"Actually, I've had a few thoughts about how we could entice more animals in," said Pie. "I used to work for the department for the protection of mythical beasts and – "

"The only thing for it is to make sure that the animals don't leave again," interrupted Gertrude.

Pie noticed that she was holding a long rope, a heavy chain and a large hammer. Whatever she was planning, it was unlikely to be in line with his view that animals should be shown respect.

Later that day, a huge lumbering hippophant ambled through one of the larger holes and started munching its way through a bowl of porridge. Gertrude snuck up behind it and wrapped the chain around its neck, then hastily tied the other end around a tree.

The startled animal reared up and bolted, yanking the tree clean out of the ground.

"Hm, I need a bigger tree," said Gertrude.

"Or a smaller animal," replied Pie, who was relieved the plan hadn't worked.

However, the next day Gertrude was successful. Pie discovered a beautiful grey horse with a magnificent set of wings. It looked rather distressed, having been lassoed and tied to a tree.

Pie argued his case with Gertrude. "You can't tie Lightning to a tree. Flying horses are extremely sensitive."

"Lightning?" she replied.

"Yes, I named her that because of the white mark on her head."

"I like that. Yes, we'll put that on a flyer. But I'm sorry. There's no question of releasing her. The tourists will come flooding now we've got Lightning the Wonder Horse!"

However, no tourist ever got a chance to meet Lightning because, that night, Pie snuck back into the park and released the flying horse.

Watching Lightning's huge wings flapping as she flew up and away, Pie became aware he wasn't alone. He turned to find a young witch behind him.

"Agnes!" he said. "How's life as the king's magical advisor?"

"Up and down. The king needs you. The city is in danger," she replied.

"Oh good," said Pie, "because I think I've just lost another job."

Lightning the Wonder Horse!

Visit Wildlife Safari Park to see our latest attraction …

Bring this flyer for a 10% discount to see our wonderful flyer.

Chapter 2

The Golden Lamp of Kabbam

Pie and Agnes chatted as they made their way through the bustling city to the palace.

"How's the magic going?" asked Pie.

"Good, I made this last week." Agnes pulled out a small bottle of green liquid.

"What is it?"

"Enlarging potion. One drop will make a cucumber the size of a canoe. Imagine, we could feed the whole city."

"With cucumber?" said Pie.

Agnes scowled. "And other things. Except I need the king's permission and he only wants to make larger cakes for his parties."

They reached the palace gates where two guards uncrossed their spears and saluted. On top of Pie's hat was his pet mouse, Mantini, who stood on her hindlegs and saluted back.

"Come on," said Agnes. "The king is in the command room with Commander Nelson."

They climbed the stairs of a tower and entered the circular room. In the centre was a table with a detailed model of the whole kingdom. The king and Commander Nelson stood around the table.

"Ah, Pie!" cried Commander Nelson.

"What kind? Apple, blueberry?" The king turned around. "Oh, I see. Hello."

"What's going on?" asked Pie.

"Elephants!" yelled Commander Nelson, using a long stick to push a pile of elephant figurines towards the city. "We've just heard that the Armed Elephant Clan are marching upon the Great City."

"Right. So, what's the plan?" said Pie. "From my time as an army advisor, I'd say the best place to ambush them would be – "

"We don't have quite enough troops for an ambush," blustered Commander Nelson.

"Why? How many do you have?" asked Pie.

"At this present moment, right now, as we speak … between three and four."

"Three or four hundred? Thousand?"

"No ... Three or four soldiers," admitted the commander. "It depends on whether Brian is feeling better. He has a poorly tummy."

"How has this happened?" cried Pie.

"I believe it was some dodgy prawns," replied the commander.

"I meant, what happened to the rest of the army?" stated Pie, exasperated.

"I might be partly responsible for that," said the king. "You see, I had an argument with the queen about whether the world was flat or round."

"It's round," said Pie.

"That's what the mapmakers tell us, but how can we be sure? That was my point.

Anyway, we had this disagreement, so I sent the army to go and find the edge of the world to prove me right."

"Why would you send the entire army to find the edge of the world?"

"They were just sitting around doing nothing. The thing is, with armies, when there's no war on, there's really not much for them to do."

"How long ago was this?"

"The week before last," admitted the king. "Still, if you're right, they'll be back … at some point." The king optimistically glanced out of the window.

"So how are we going to stop the city from being flattened by elephants?" asked Pie.

"I have the solution to that," said Agnes. "I've been spending a lot of time in the library, researching magic, and I've discovered the location of the Golden Lamp of Kabbam."

"The famous lamp containing an all-powerful genie who will grant three wishes?!" exclaimed Pie. "I thought that was just a story."

"Just because it's a story, it doesn't mean it isn't true," replied Agnes.

She reached into her cloak and pulled out a large book. It landed with a thud on the table, knocking over several toy elephants. While Commander Nelson fussed about getting them to stand upright, Agnes turned to a page she'd folded over. It contained a map of Mile Isle. Below this was a poem.
Agnes read it out.

Up the jagged cliff, you'll climb,
Down the half a hole, you'll drop,
Along the pitch-black tunnel,
Beware the sudden stop.
Across the threadbare bridge,
Be careful not to stamp.
Into the chamber of treasure,
Where you will find the lamp.

"Your mission," said the king, "is to follow these instructions, get the lamp and bring it back here so that I can rub it and use one of my wishes to save the city. Obviously, once I've done that, I'll have two more wishes. I was thinking of wishing for a really large cake. Or perhaps a cake that grows back every time you take a bite. Imagine that."

"How long have we got?" asked Pie.

"If my information is correct, the armoured elephants will be upon us before the week is out." Commander Nelson lifted up an elephant figurine and made a trumpeting noise.

"Who else is coming on this mission?" asked Pie.

"Just you two," said the king. "We don't have anyone else."

"Oh yes, you do." A young man with tins and pans tied to his belt clattered into the room.

"Claymore!" said Pie. "What have you been up to?"

"Well, I *should* be leading the army. After all, my combat skills are second to none …"
He demonstrated by waving a ladle and a pot about a bit. "However, the king decided to put me in the royal kitchen washing up."

The king smiled and said,
"Good washer-uppers are hard to find. The last one kept leaving smudges on the glasses."

"Your majesty," said Pie. "I request that we take Claymore on this mission. After all, we're going to need all the help we can get if we are to find this genie and save the city."

"Oh, very well, and you can take my Express Coach. Tell Stable Master Higgins to attach my fastest horses," said the king. "Nelson, you'll have to do the washing up until Claymore returns."

"But I'm the commander of your armies," protested Commander Nelson.

"Never mind that," harrumphed the king. "Go and find a tea towel."

The Kingdom of Mirthia

The Great City – surrounded by *Lovely Woodland*

Mile Isle

Big Pond Lake is to the west where the Trout Tickling Tribes live on a floating village.

Cloud Mountains
in the east, inhabited by
the *Armed Elephant Clan*

Beware bandits!

(The village of) *Rather*
(at the base of) *Done Hill*,
(beside the river) *Bottom*

Chapter 3
Big Chicken Express

Pie, Claymore and Agnes arrived at the door of the royal stables, where a bearded man in a red jacket stood outside. He held a whip in one hand. His other hand was resting on a golden coach with large shiny wheels and a red stripe down the side.

"Are you Stable Master Higgins?" asked Pie.

"Aye, I'm Higgins."

"Is this the Express Coach?" said Agnes.

"Aye, that it be."

Claymore whistled, clearly impressed. "How fast does it go?"

"That depends on how many horses you have pulling it," said Higgins.

"We urgently need six of your fastest stallions," said Pie.

"Ah, that might be a problem," replied Higgins. "They've all gone. Migrated most likely."

The stable master pushed open the doors to reveal that every stable was empty. The only living thing was a chicken, quietly pecking the ground.

"Horses don't migrate," said Pie.

"That's what I thought," said Higgins. "But they've all gone. Not just from the stables but from the whole city. There's not a horse for miles around. Not even a little one."

"A foal," corrected Pie.

"How dare you. I'm no one's fool," said Higgins. "Still, hopefully, they'll migrate back in the spring."

"How could they even get out?" asked Pie.

"They must have opened the doors, I suppose," said Higgins. "They're very intelligent animals, horses."

"Isn't it more likely that our enemies snuck into the stables and stole the horses, making the Great City utterly defenceless against attack?" said Pie.

Higgins looked at the empty stable, then down at the chicken. "Now you mention it, it did seem odd that they all vanished ... without leaving a note or anything."

Pie shook his head in despair then picked up the chicken.

"What are you doing with Marjorie Feathers?" asked Higgins.

"She's going to help us get to the coast," said Pie. "Agnes, we'll need your potion."

Pie placed the chicken in the middle of the coach harness and stood back. Agnes leant over and tipped the bottle, careful only to allow one drop to land on the chicken's head.

"Step back," she said.

"Why?" asked Claymore. "What's going to happen?"

With an almighty SQUAWK! the chicken suddenly grew to the size of a large bull. It looked confused for a moment, then went back to pecking. Its huge beak now created enormous holes in the ground. Claymore quickly ensured that the chicken was properly attached, then leapt into the driver's seat and pulled back on the reins. The chicken reared back.

"All aboard the Big Chicken Express!" cried Claymore.

Once Claymore got the hang of the reins, Marjorie turned out to be an excellent runner, pulling the coach faster than six horses. The journey passed in a flurry of massive feathers and huge eggs, which went rolling down the road. They gave the chicken an extra boost as they were ejected.

"Just imagine the omelette," said Claymore, his eyes wide.

"They are eggs-tremely large," said Agnes.

"If you boiled one, you could dip actual soldiers in it," added Pie.

Due to the unusually quiet roads, they reached the coast in a matter of hours. On the outskirts of town, they saw a sign with a skull and crossbones.

Malarkey Bay: Beware, Pirates Be Here!

"Woah there, Marjorie." Claymore yanked on the reins and the chicken slowed down to a trot as they passed a row of shops.

All of the shopkeepers wore bandannas and baggy shirts.

"I'd heard this place attracted pirates, but this is ridiculous," said Pie.

"There are a lot of pirates," said Agnes.

"Yes, there arrrr," joked Claymore.

"At least that should make finding a boat easy enough," said Pie.

Claymore steered Marjorie down to a wooden jetty, where a lone pirate stood selling exquisitely carved wooden parrots. Claymore tied the oversized chicken to a wooden post.

"Excuse me," said Pie.

"Aye, lad," said the pirate. "Would ye like to buy one of me pretty polly talking parrots?" She picked one up, then spoke out of the side of her mouth, pretending it was the toy talking. "Who's a pretty boy then?"

"Er, no. We need a ship to take us over to Mile Isle." Pie pointed to the island just off the coast.

"A ship?" said the pirate. "You'll be lucky."

"But isn't this town full of pirates?" said Pie.

"Not real pirates," said the pirate.

"What do you mean?" asked Agnes.

"We discovered years ago that most folk didn't want to see *actual* pirates. They just wanted to have fun with the *idea* of pirates. So we swapped piracy for tourism. I used to be a carpenter repairing ships, but there's no call for that anymore so I make these instead." She waggled a wooden parrot and squawked, "Polly want a cracker."

"No army, no horses. And now, no ships," said Pie. "This whole kingdom is falling apart."

"Actually," continued the pretend pirate, "now I think about it, old Captain Bushybeard has a boat at the end of the jetty."

"Is he a real pirate?" asked Pie.

"Sort of. He's an ex-pirate," said the woman, squawking and waggling the parrot.

They all traipsed along the jetty. There they found a clean-shaven man, leaning back, wearing a colourful shirt and shorts, and holding a fishing rod between his toes.

"Excuse me. We're looking for Captain Bushybeard," said Pie.

"Aye, that be me," said the man.

"Where's your beard?" asked Claymore.

"I sold it," he replied. "Along with my jacket, my jewellery, my boots and my cutlass. Oh, and my ship."

"Can you row us over to Mile Isle?" said Pie.

"No problem at all," said Captain Bushybeard. "I was going to head out that way anyway on a fishing trip. Hop aboard."

BREAKING NEWS!

The Mirthia Observer
Tomorrow's News Today!

EGGS-TRA! EGGS-TRA! EXTRA LARGE!

Villagers were shell-shocked today when several large chicken eggs caused havoc. Farmer, Brian Kindling, said, "One was the size of my house. It almost knocked my cow right over. It's beyond a yoke."

EAKING NEWS!

Not everyone was so clucky. Eggs-traordinary chaos followed as houses were flattened, crops were crushed, fences were smashed and villagers scrambled over each other, hoping to scoop up a free egg dinner. The origin of the eggs is unknown, although there have been reports of a very large chicken pulling a coach along the eastern highway.

Chapter 4
The half a hole

Captain Bushybeard rowed too slowly for Pie's liking, but he was more than happy to hand the oars to Claymore and let him take over. Agnes steered, while the smooth-chinned ex-pirate leant back with his hands behind his head and entertained them with stories of his adventures on the high seas.

"I've actually started writing my life story," he said, as they drew closer to the island. "Apparently, pirate memoirs are very popular at the moment. Of course, all those celebrity pirates get the big booty. I've been struggling with the title though."

"What about *I, Aye*?" asked Pie.

"Or *Bushybeard, a Close Shave*," suggested Agnes.

They spent the rest of the journey suggesting names for Bushybeard's book.

When they reached Mile Isle, they looked up at the sharp cliffs that rose from the sea. Seagulls circled above. Waves crashed onto jagged rocks below.

"Is there a path to take us up?" asked Pie.

"No," replied Captain Bushybeard. "The only way up is to scale the cliffs."

"Up the jagged cliff, you'll climb," said Agnes, remembering the instructions from the book.

Bushybeard took the oars back and rowed them close enough so that all three could jump onto the rock.

It wasn't an easy climb. The chalk cliffside was as jagged as it was crumbly. Considering how dangerous it was, they were surprised to see lots of goats happily grazing on the grass that grew on the cliffside.

Eventually, with scuffed knees and aching hands, they reached the top. They all stood and looked back across the sea.

"Wow, you can see all the way to the Great City from here," said Claymore.

"And beyond," said Agnes. "Look, the Armed Elephant Clan are getting closer."

Huge clouds of dust rose as the thundering army charged towards the Great City.

"They haven't reached the woods yet, but they will soon," said Pie. "What's the next part of the instructions?"

"Down the half a hole, you'll drop," said Agnes.

"What is half a hole?" asked Claymore.

"Let's see if we can find out," replied Pie.

They turned and searched the clifftop until they became aware of a frantic bleating sound. They approached and saw one of the mountain goats trapped. Its head and two back legs were visible, but its back half was out of sight.

"It's stuck in a hole," said Claymore. "Fear not. I shall rescue it."

He grabbed the horns and yanked as hard as he could, but the goat remained lodged. It bleated louder.

"There's strange magic at work here," said Agnes. "This must be the half a hole. Anything that steps into it will neither fall through nor walk over but become lodged, half in, half out."

"So how do we get the goat out and us through?" asked Claymore.

"We'll have to make the hole bigger," said Agnes.

"So that the half a hole is a whole hole," said Pie.

"I'll get to it." Claymore whipped out a pair of large spoons and set about digging around the goat. Once the half a hole was twice its former size, a confused look crossed the goat's face. With an alarmed bleat, it suddenly fell through.

Claymore peered into the hole. "Do you think he'll be all right?"

"Let's hope so, because we're going down too," said Pie.

He jumped into the hole. Agnes did the same. Claymore clipped his spoons back onto his belt and followed.

Plummeting down, it felt like a helter-skelter! One by one, they landed on top of each other, with the poor bewildered goat at the bottom. They all got to their feet.

Burning torches attached to jagged cave walls provided flickering light.

"We're inside the island," said Pie.

The goat bleated and ran down one of the tunnels that disappeared into darkness.

Pie pulled one of the torches off the wall and waved it around. "So which passageway do we take?"

"Along the pitch-black tunnel," said Agnes, recalling the instructions from her book.

"They're all dark," said Claymore.

"I've got an idea," said Agnes. "Pie, step into one of the tunnels."

Pie did as he was instructed and instantly the flame from his torch lit up the rock walls.

"Now, try the others," urged Agnes.

Pie entered each tunnel in turn. When he stepped inside the fourth tunnel, no shadows appeared and the light from the flame died down. The tunnel remained dark.

"Magic," whispered Claymore.

"Come on. This way." Pie placed one hand on the wall and felt his way along.

It was a long and uncertain journey through the tunnel, with lots of tripping and apologising. Pie led the way, repeating the next line of the instructions to himself.

"Beware the sudden stop," he kept muttering. "Beware the sudden – "

Pie stumbled. He would have fallen had Agnes not grabbed his arm. The torch in his hand was suddenly glowing again. They had reached the end of the dark tunnel and were standing at the edge of a sheer drop. A rickety bridge hung by a thread across a ravine.

On the other side was the entrance to a room that sparkled with the promise of treasure.

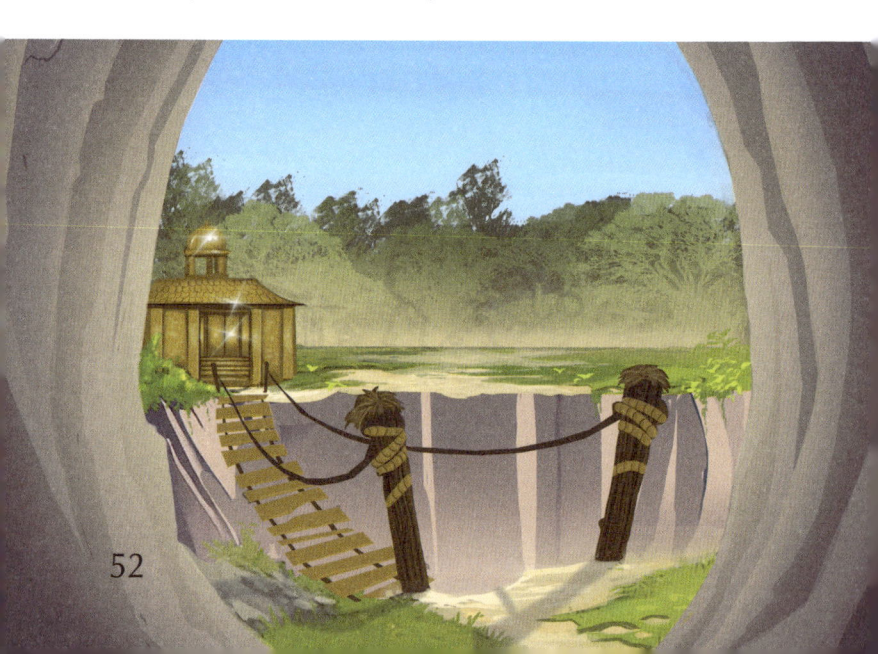

"The lamp must be in there!" said Pie.

"Across the threadbare bridge, be careful not to stamp," said Agnes.

"Never mind stamping," said Claymore. "If any of us so much as steps on that thing, it will collapse."

Pie picked up a stone and dropped it. They listened until eventually they heard a distant splash.

"I don't fancy falling down there, it seems the ravine goes all the way down to the ocean," said Agnes. "But Claymore is right. There's no way that bridge will take our weight."

"Not ours," said Pie, "but I know someone who will be able to get across."

"Who?" asked the others.

"Mantini," he replied.

"Ta-da!" cried the mouse.

Captain Bushybeard's memoir

Chapter 1: From Cabin Boy to Captain

As a lad, I always ~~dreimpt~~ ~~drenit~~ dreamt of travelling the world. And although I did make that childhood dream come true, I do have some regrets. For all the treasure I have acquired, this is a story of loss .... an eye, a hand, a couple of parrots, three ships, several treasure maps and more shipmates than I can count.

55

Chapter 5

What goes down must go up

"Will Mantini be able to carry the lamp?" asked Agnes, watching the mouse scurry across the rickety bridge.

"Oh yes, back in her circus days, she was the bottom half of an acrobatic act. She never had any problem carrying her partner," said Pie.

"I think that lamp might be a bit heavier than a mouse," said Claymore.

"Her partner was a cat," Pie smiled.

When Mantini reached the other side, she glanced back.

"Good job," called Pie. "Now grab the lamp and get back as soon as you can."

They watched as Mantini crossed the room, then scrambled up a plinth. She slipped her tail through the lamp's handle, then made her way down.

There was a rumbling sound and the plinth began to disappear into the ground. Mantini picked up the pace as glistening golden artefacts crashed down on her, clattering to the ground.

She'd only just made it out of the room, when the ceiling collapsed. The others watched from across the ravine, unable to help.

"Quick, back across the – "

But before Pie could finish his sentence, the last remaining rope snapped and the bridge fell away. All three stared in horror as the bridge plummeted down into the ocean below.

"What do we do now?" asked Claymore.

"We'll have to jump," said Pie.

"Jump?!" exclaimed Claymore.

"He's right," replied Agnes. "This place is collapsing. The only way is down."

"Mantini!" yelled Pie. "On my count, jump into the ravine."

Mantini looked down at the ravine.

"One … Two … Three … JUMP!"

They all leapt into the ravine. Pie caught Mantini and the lamp mid-air as they plummeted down.

"Rub the lamp!" yelled Claymore.

"The king said not to!" yelled Pie.

"He hadn't just jumped off a cliff!" screamed Agnes.

Pie rubbed the lamp. Yellow smoke shot out from the spout and created a cloud cushion which caught them all. Claymore peered over the edge and saw the sea, crashing onto the rocks below.

"The genie is appearing," said Agnes.

Strands from the cloud twisted up and formed the top half of a man, with his bulging arms crossed.

"Hello, I am the almighty genie," boomed the voice.

"Hi," said Pie. "We're glad you're here because – "

"This is a recorded message," continued the genie.

"Wait. What?!" said Pie.

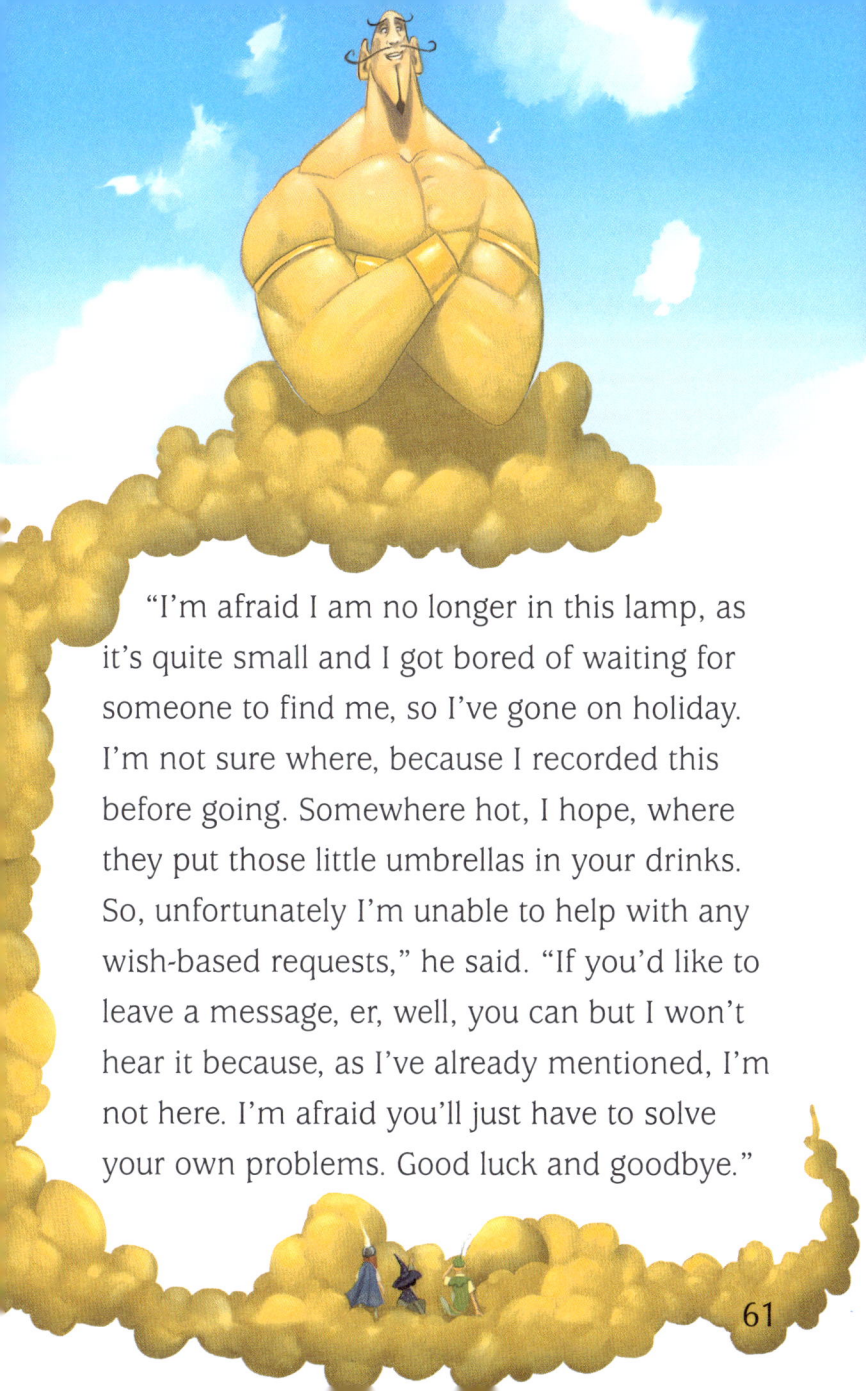

"I'm afraid I am no longer in this lamp, as it's quite small and I got bored of waiting for someone to find me, so I've gone on holiday. I'm not sure where, because I recorded this before going. Somewhere hot, I hope, where they put those little umbrellas in your drinks. So, unfortunately I'm unable to help with any wish-based requests," he said. "If you'd like to leave a message, er, well, you can but I won't hear it because, as I've already mentioned, I'm not here. I'm afraid you'll just have to solve your own problems. Good luck and goodbye."

As quickly as it had appeared, the genie and the cloud vanished. Pie, Claymore, Agnes, Mantini and the lamp all crashed down into the icy sea. It was a shock to the system, but they soon bobbed back up above the waves.

"We need to swim back towards the island," yelled Pie.

"Where's the lamp?" asked Agnes.

"I dropped it," said Pie.

When they climbed out of the sea onto the rocks, they caught their breath.

"So we went all this way for an empty lamp that's now at the bottom of the ocean," said Claymore. "And if that's not bad enough, we're stranded on an island and unable to prevent an army of elephants trampling the Great City!"

"If I learnt anything from my job as a proverb writer," said Pie, "it's that when you've hit rock bottom, there really is only one way to go … up."

"But how can we go anywhere?" said Agnes, wringing her robes. "Claymore's right. It's hopeless."

"Not at all. Look. Lightning."

Claymore and Agnes looked up, confused.

"It doesn't look stormy to me," said Claymore.

"Not lightning as in thunder and lightning. Lightning! Hey, down here!" Pie whistled and waved his arms as a magnificent, winged horse burst through the clouds and zoomed down.

"Wow!" said Claymore.

There wasn't enough room for the horse to land, but she flew so low that her hooves skimmed the water, sending it spraying up, and creating a rainbow in the sunlight. She followed this with an impressive loop-the-loop.

"She wants us to jump on," said Pie. "Get ready."

"Are you sure about this?" asked Agnes, nervously. "Flying horses don't usually allow riders."

"This one's a friend," said Pie, grabbing Mantini and popping her onto his head. "Also, it's the only way to get off this island and save the Great City."

Lightning flew low so they could reach her, but they all knew that the smallest mistake would send them back into the icy cold water.

"Here goes nothing!" cried Pie.

The three heroes leapt and landed on the horse's back. As soon as they were on, Lightning tipped her wings and rocketed back up into the blue sky.

With no saddle, it wasn't the easiest of horse rides, but soon enough Lightning was flying smoothly above the clouds.

"Watch out!" Agnes ducked and narrowly avoided a collision with a pigeon.

"Look where you're going next time, Mr Flaps," yelled Claymore at the poor confused pigeon.

"Now all we need to do is head back and save the city from an army of elephants," said Pie.

"But how can we?" said Claymore. "The lamp was empty and all we have is us three, one mouse and a flying horse."

"You forgot the most important thing. We have a plan," replied Pie.

Mantini's act

The Incredible "Cat and Mouse" Acrobats …

Mantini and Mister Mittens

Marvel as cat
catches mouse

And then mouse
catches cat!

Chapter 6

The enor-mouse

The strong wind and huge beating wings made it a challenge for Pie, Claymore and Agnes to cling on, but the winged horse flew fast. It wasn't long before they were soaring over the Great City.

The Armed Elephant Clan had reached the edge of the woods near the city. They charged forward at full pelt, trampling over trees and crushing everything in their way with their huge thundering feet.

"So, what's the plan?" asked Claymore. "You want me to drop down and give those elephants the old double pan wallop?"

"Claymore, in terms of fighting skills with kitchenware, there's no one better," said Pie, "but even you might struggle against an entire army of elephants."

"Then what?" asked Claymore.

"I need you to do some rounding up."

"Oh, really? I was never very good at maths."

Pie laughed. "Not rounding up numbers. Rounding up horses. Look down there."

Claymore was surprised to see that the field at the foot of the mountains was crammed full of horses. "They didn't migrate very far," he said.

"They didn't migrate at all," retorted Pie. "As I suspected, our enemies took them and are keeping them trapped in that field. I need you to open the gate and lead them all back to the city where they belong."

"You can rely on me, Pie," said Claymore.

"Lightning, can you bring us down to drop Claymore off?" said Pie, patting the horse.

"There's no time for that," said Claymore. "See you back at the city."

With that, Claymore leapt off the flying horse and plummeted down.

"Noooo, it's too high!" cried Agnes.

To both her and Pie's astonishment, a patchwork parachute flew up from one of Claymore's pans, allowing him to glide safely down to the ground.

"I do believe that's a parachute made of dishcloths," said Agnes. "So, what next?"

"Now we'll need the rest of your enlarging potion," said Pie.

"But what can you make bigger that will scare off all those elephants?" asked Agnes.

"The one thing that all elephants are afraid of," replied Pie, with a tap of his hat.

——*—*—*

73

In the Great City, the king had called an emergency meeting. He sat at the head of a long table, as each advisor took turns to offer their views on the best course of action.

"To sum up," said Commander Nelson. "Pie and his team must have failed in their mission and, with no horses, we are unable to flee. Therefore, I advise the following strategy." He unravelled a large piece of parchment detailing his plan. "Stage one, quake. Stage two, whimper. Stage three, cry. And finally, stage four ... plead."

"Interesting. Please could you expand on that?" asked the king.

"Of course." Commander Nelson took a long stick and pointed at each bullet point. "Firstly, we quake in our boots. Then we whimper, possibly under a table, maybe behind a curtain."

"I've been whimpering for a while now," said a bearded baron.

"Oh, me too," agreed everyone around the table.

"Good work," said Commander Nelson. "Crying should follow. And then, when the enemy has stormed our defences and has us up against the wall, we unveil our master plan, and plead for our lives."

"That all sounds splendid to me," said the king. "Let's put this plan into action."

A sudden jolt interrupted them.

"Oh no, the elephants are upon us already," wailed a bald bishop.

"No, look!" said a pageboy, pointing out of the window.

Everyone rushed to see.

"Out of my way. Out of my way." The king pushed through. When he saw the cause of the tremors, he gasped. "Well, I never."

Standing in front of the army of armoured elephants was a mouse the size of a mountain, its whiskers as long as tree trunks, and its tail snaking all the way to the city walls.

"TAAAAA-DAAAAAH!" roared Mantini.

Flying around the enormous mouse's head, a winged horse carried two brave heroes.

They all stared in wonder at this remarkable spectacle, until the door was flung open and Stable Master Higgins burst in.

"The horses are returning," he yelled. "Young Master Claymore is bringing them into the city through the south gate."

"We're saved," said the king.

"Yes, well done us," said Commander Nelson. "I knew our plan would work."

——*—*—*

Pie tugged lightly on Lightning's mane, and they circled around to see Claymore leading the horses back to the city.

"We did it," said Agnes.

"And without any help from a genie," said Pie.

Lightning dipped her wings and soared down. Pie and Agnes clung on tight, but when Lightning came to a sudden stop on the ground, she sent them both flying into a bush.

Pie looked up and saw that Lightning was happily munching hay from a feeder on the east side of the Great City's Wildlife Safari Park. Thankfully, there was no sign of Gertrude.

"So, how do we make Mantini mouse-sized again?" asked Pie.

"Ah, well, I'll have to make shrinking potion," replied Agnes. "I just need a few ingredients."

"No problem. We can pop by the market," said Pie.

Agnes coughed. "The thing is, they're not really the sort of things you can easily buy. We need an ogre's toenail, the eyelash of a wood sprite and a couple of magic beans – "

Pie smiled. "So another quest. I guess I've nothing better to do. Besides, now we've got Lightn—"

Pie was interrupted by the sound of flapping wings and whinnying, as the flying horse took to the sky and flew away.

"Oh. Never mind." Pie sighed. "Let's go and find Claymore."

And so Pie Fortune and his friends set off on another adventure.

But that's another story for another time.

The End

81

Commander Nelson's Brilliant Defence Plan

QUAKE – quivering is also an option

WHIMPER – as quietly as you can

CRY – as loudly as possible

PLEAD – If your enemy has witnessed the quaking, whimpering and crying, it's time to deploy the big guns and … beg for life.

Captain Bushybeard's notebook

Ideas for my memoir book title ...

Me, Myself and Eye-Patch!

My aarrgh-tobiography

Things I need to get off my chest

Life is Bootyful

The Aaarrrt of Piracy

I Think, Therefore I Arr

Captain Bushybeard: My Story

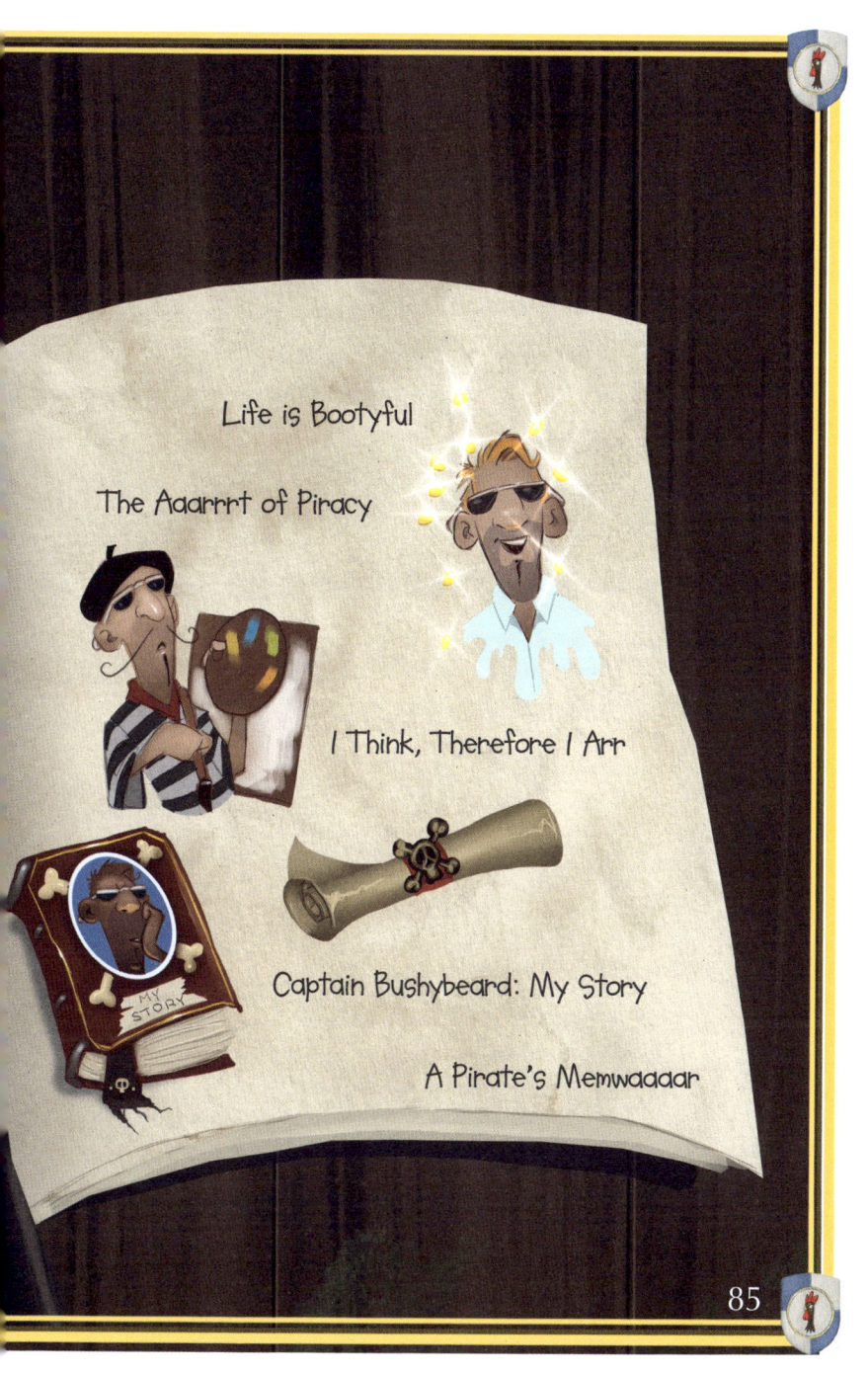

A Pirate's Memwaaaar

About the author

What do you like most about writing?

I like creating things. I'm not very good at DIY. I can't put up shelves or build cabinets, but I am good at using my imagination and making up stories and songs. I enjoy starting out with an idea and finding out where it leads.

Gareth P Jones

How did you come up with the idea for this story?

I started with the title. Pie Fortune books always involve a quest and I like the idea of genies. But then I had the idea that the genie would be a red herring. As I started writing, I kept my eye open for clues about what would happen. I wrote the whole thing very roughly, then my computer died and I lost everything. I then had to rewrite the whole thing, which was much harder than I was expecting it to be. But eventually I did it. Then I edited the book and made it better before sending it off. In terms of the setting, I looked at the map that Dan the illustrator did for the last book. I realised there was an unnamed island, so I named it Mile Isle.

Which character do you most relate to and why?

I like Pie. He is resourceful and optimistic. He's a problem-solver. I want to be like that. Sometimes I am like that. But not always.

Did you have a favourite scene to write?

I really struggled with the ending when Mantini is made larger. But when I hit upon the idea of switching perspective and going back to the king and his useless advisors, I knew I could make it work. I love writing the bits with the king because he's self-important and utterly useless and his scenes always make me chuckle.

If you could be any character from the book for a day, who would you choose and why?

In this book, I think I would enjoy a day as Captain Bushybeard, the retired pirate. I'd enjoy bobbing about on the sea in my little boat thinking about all the adventures I used to have. But, I'd be safe in the knowledge that no one would try to make me walk the plank.

What do you hope readers will get out of the book?

I hope they laugh and want to read another Pie Fortune story because I'd like to write the next one now.

About the illustrator

What did you like best about illustrating this book?

I love illustrating new characters – it's my favourite thing to do. I get to experiment with different shapes and facial expressions. It is so easy when they are hilarious and that is what appeals to me about Gareth as an author. He has a great way of describing a character, so much so you can easily imagine them in your head. And of course illustrating humour, it's just the best. Those things combined is a winning formula for me. On more than a few occasions, I found myself chuckling away while I was drawing.

Dan Whisker

What was the most difficult thing about illustrating this book?

For me, the most difficult thing about this book is the colouring, because I can get so carried away with the detail, I make things hard for myself. I also found it hard to finish because I was having great fun. It is difficult to say goodbye sometimes!

Who's your favourite character in the story? How did you decide what they should look like?

My favourite character is Captain Bushybeard. It seems nothing fazes him – he takes life in his stride and just chills out with whatever he is doing. To me that sounds like bliss! It was easy to decide what he looks like as he is described well and his approach to life is something that appeals very strongly to me.

What magical creature would you like to have as a pet?

I would say probably a Unicorn-Chihuahua, one of my favourite fantasy beasts combined with my favourite pet (which I have three of … Chihuahua's that is).

If you had a magic lamp, what would you wish for?

Unlike most people, who might say money and wealth, I would wish for a lovely island. I would want it in the middle of a huge lake, surrounded by tall mountains where I can keep all my Unicorn-Chihuahua's (Unihuahua's I guess?). Also, a tropical shirt and a rowing boat – not too much to ask for, I don't think.

Book chat

Have you read any other books like this?

If you could ask the author one question, what would you ask?

What was your favourite part of the book and why?

Who is your favourite character and why?

What do you think Pie, Agnes and Claymore learnt from this adventure?

What different skills do each of the characters bring to the problems they face?

Would you read another book that followed on from this one? What do you think should be in it?

Would you recommend this book? Why or why not?

Book challenge:
Design your own golden lamp and write down three wishes you'd ask a genie.

Collins
BIG CAT

Published by Collins
An imprint of HarperCollins*Publishers*

The News Building
1 London Bridge Street
London SE1 9GF
UK

Macken House
39/40 Mayor Street Upper
Dublin 1
D01 C9W8
Ireland

Text © Gareth P Jones 2024
Design and illustrations © HarperCollins*Publishers* Limited 2024

10 9 8 7 6 5 4 3 2 1

ISBN 978-0-00-868112-8

All rights reserved. No part of this publication may be reproduced, stored in a retrieval system, or transmitted in any form by any means, electronic, mechanical, photocopying, recording or otherwise, without the prior written permission of the Publisher or a licence permitting restricted copying in the United Kingdom issued by the Copyright Licensing Agency Ltd, 5th Floor, Shackleton House, 4 Battle Bridge Lane, London SE1 2HX.

British Library Cataloguing-in-Publication Data
A catalogue record for this publication is available from the British Library.

Download the teaching notes and word cards to accompany this book at:
http://littlewandle.org.uk/signupfluency/

Get the latest Collins Big Cat news at
collins.co.uk/collinsbigcat

Author: Gareth P Jones
Illustrator: Dan Whisker (The Bright Agency)
Publisher: Laura White
Product manager and
  commissioning editor: Caroline Green
Series editor: Charlotte Raby
Development editor: Catherine Baker
Project manager: Emily Hooton
Copyeditor: Sally Byford
Proofreader: Catherine Dakin
Cover designer: Sarah Finan
Typesetter: 2Hoots Publishing Services Ltd
Production controller: Katharine Willard

Printed in the UK.

MIX
Paper | Supporting responsible forestry
FSC™ C007454

This book is produced from independently certified FSC™ paper to ensure responsible forest management.

For more information visit: www.harpercollins.co.uk/green

Made with responsibly sourced paper and vegetable ink

Scan to see how we are reducing our environmental impact.